A JOURNE   )

Collected Poems 1945-2016

Helen Pinkerton

Wiseblood Books

Newberg, Oregon

Published by Wiseblood Books
www.wisebloodbooks.com

Cover: Dominic Heisdorf
Editorial Assistant: Amelia Kumpel

Printed in the United States of America
Set in Arabic Typesetting

Library of Congress Cataloging-in-Publication Data
Pinkerton, Helen, 1927-
A Journey of the Mind: Collected Poems 1946-
2016/ Helen Pinkerton;
1. Pinkerton, Helen, 1927-
2. Poetry

ISBN-13: 978-0615933115
ISBN-10: 0615933114

TABLE OF CONTENTS

I
NEW POEMS

METAPHYSICAL SONG

First principle,
Being's pure act,
Infinite cause
Of finite fact,

Essential being,
Beyond our sight,
Without which, nothing,
Neither love nor light,

Only through You
Love's infinite power
Brings into being
Atom and flower.

Only through You,
Infinite light
Illuminates
Both seen and sight,

Beckoning us,
Alert, awake,
Along the way
That we must take,

Resting in this:
The journey's true,
First, midst, and last,
Grounded in You.

Coronach for Christopher Drummond

By lamp or morning light,
Bent close over the page,
You heard the language right,
No matter from what age.

Whether Jonson's grieving prayers,
Or Milton's rich designs,
Or Melville's rugged verse,
Or Winters' densest lines,

Your mind knew the intent,
Your voice wakened the sound—
The sleeping beauty pent
In chambers underground.

Surrounded now by noise,
My words, that sought your praise,
Your understanding voice,
Confront the silent days.

THE OLD POET: MARGARET PRESTON REMEMBERS

Lexington, Virginia, July 21, 1891

The old talk to themselves or with their dead,
As I, sitting alone with you, my dear,
Not seeing much, nor hearing any voices
This day of days, when they again assemble
At Thomas's grave to honor him, as when,
So long ago, I saw our soldiers come
(Even some of theirs though still the enemy)
To mark his grave with gathered flowers and leaves—
Fit tribute of the brave man to the brave.
Soon they will fire the cannon, a peaceful
    signal,
And not as once, stopped in the orchard sun,
Or in a garden row or quiet street,
I heard it like a dry and distant thunder,
Sounding over the Blue Ridge haze from fields—
Manassas, Winchester, and Chancellorsville—
Where Thomas taught them how a soldier fights.
I'll not be there today to hear his praises;
Someone will read my own old ode for him.
I did not have the heart to write a new one.
I shall sit here with you, remembering him,
As only you and I and Ellie knew him,
Just as he was when we were young together,
The few short years he lived in my father's house.
Earnest and ardent, so precise in speech,
Yet with a cheek that colored with delight
When Elinor embraced him and consented;

12

With eyes that shone with laughter at my wit.
Afterward came the terrible year: lost wife,
Lost sister, the child who never breathed, and then
Beloved Mother, after long pain and fever.
Our painful healing, month by month: shared faith,
Shared books, and hours of deep wide-ranging talk.
Stories and laughter took the place of mourning.
Perfect his resignation; mine was not.
You knew, of course, I loved him and he, me,
As much as one can love, without a hope
To marry. Separation cooled the flame.
He traveled, met Anna, and I, dear John, found you.
Thereafter, never a day shadowed our love,
Not even war with all its absences.
Your daughters became my daughters, your sons my
    sons,
And our two boys then crowned our kingdom's joy.
      There. There. I feel the gun's salute again,
Might hear the applause and shouting for our
    Thomas,
The dear dead *Major*, as we called him then,
The storied *Stonewall* as the world soon knew him—
Might hear, were my ears sharp as they once were
When I heard guns at thirty miles or more
Sounded again at Manassas on the field,
Where later you found William's shallow grave,
His golden hair crumbled, matted with dirt,
His fair expressive face despoiled of features.
You knew him only by his soldier's shirt,
Where I, good seamstress, had embroidered his
    name.
You covered him with our Virginia earth.

The nation heals itself. You felt it would,
Even mid-war when northern infantry
To honor Thomas, walked to his unmarked grave.
Fighting, you shared our goal of revolution,
Though I perceived you doubted our success.
My loss was sure: father, brothers, and sisters
Estranged from me, my memories of home
Expunged by war. And he, who taught me Greek,
The love of truth, and skills that enrich the mind—
He wiped Virginia's dust from his carriage wheels
Believing the Union held millennial hope,
Would bring the reign of Christ to all the world.
Even after it was over, on his return,
His righteousness meeting your mild forbearance
Never lost its edge. And though he recognized
My choice was Ruth's, I wonder even now
If he forgave me. Angered by separation
From me, his grandsons, and from my mother's
    grave,
Suffering the loss of home and of his calling,
His choice severer than mine, did he at last
Discover wholeness, an unconflicted love
Before he died? We never spoke of it,
So deep, so strong was his choice for the Union.
    I carried in my heart broad northern streams,
The clean hard light of Pennsylvania's skies.
You knew my agonized, conflicted will,
And you foresaw, prophetically, our loss,
But went more bravely to the fight than zealots.
What sort of wisdom was that? This I may ask—
Now that it is no more a question, and they,

The countless graves, the lifelong crippled, the
    orphaned,
The widowed stay in my vision, fixed, relentless,
More certain than the evanescent glory.
       All this is reminiscence such as the old
Incline to and the young pardon.
But now I bring to you, my dearest friend,
A thing I cannot speak of to our children,
That only you, knowing me as you did,
And as, I dream, you do, can comprehend.
While there is time, I want to say some things
I could not say, because I could not see,
Before I lost my sight, as well as now.
When I was small, I thought perhaps there was
A place of rest for us sometime, somewhere,
Where no one called and no one cried aloud.
I sometimes thought of death as offering that.
Your God is still my God, and yet his Son,
Merciful and forgiving, now eludes me.
My sins are manifold. I feel myself
Exemplary of the seven and faith a state
I must remake each day, never a fixed
And steadfast thing like Thomas's or yours.
As each sense fails, my consciousness narrows.
A deep fear comes and not a childhood dream.
I am not ready for my death. I fear
My fear's betrayal of my long-held faith.
Nor is there anyone to comfort me.
Unless in some form God shapes for our souls
I trust that you are here, that I am heard,
In the broken conversation we call prayer.

On Taddeo di Bartolo's *Triptych of the Madonna and Child with Angel Musicians and St. John the Baptist and St. Jerome*

Her face is singularly simple, and His
Seems unaware of the inscription written
Across the scroll His hands unfold to us,
Words spoken to Moses from the burning bush:
"Ego sum Qui sum." And "Venite ad Me."
Jerome himself once said that to profess
Truly the triune mystery is to admit
We cannot comprehend it, nor does the mother,
It seems, nor Child. And yet we know the Child,

When grown to manhood, claimed again God's
    name--
"Before Abraham was I am"--baffling
Our simple minds, which try by threads and pieces
To clarify our faith, envying the ease
With which these angel choristers, with lute,
Psaltery, portative organ, and vielle,
Rejoice with their insouciant hymns of praise,
Each note a part of one felt harmony
That we would join in did we know the tune.

Yet from the pinnacle the Father and Dove
Look down, gifting with will and love the viewer,
And John, the grateful forerunner, declares:
"He Who comes after me was before me," thus
Affirming the eternal presence of the Son,
Whose timeless interaction with our time,
Can lift us undeservedly above

Time and our losses, when we rise to it.
Only His grace enables us to try,
And her simplicity is how we have to see.

And Who is God?

And Who is God? The *Is* of Abraham,
Isaac, and Jacob, self-begun *I Am*,
Actual source of act, *to-be* of being?
Or Eros, fluent in our veins, decreeing
Action and passion, will, truth or its sham?
Love's ambiguities prevent our seeing.

IRAQ: ABU GRAIB

The mass graves in the desert cry to us,
And those Saddam's pure evil would achieve.
Our failures: common sins, degraded lusts.
As impure acts, for these, also, we grieve.

TROY

No City on a Hill. A citadel,
Envied, besieged by partisans of Hell.
Beware, O Prince, some enemies inside
Dream the same dream of nihilistic pride.

II
PROMONTORY HILLS

COAST HILLSIDE

The Mondays must be lovely where you are.
All week and weekends crowds throng halls and
    gardens,
The rooms hung with the works of art you choose,
That you know best and love, though not your own
But theirs, who see or not see, as they can.
Now, in the quiet of their absence, you,
Hearing the bronze peristyle fountain plash,
Will turn, perhaps, outside your office, glance
Down marble corridor, past fluted columns,
And see me standing where I last saw you,
Where we talked of the kouros' radiant poise.

Here, wild-oat fields unfold in planes of gold—
Of green-gold, white-gold, dun, drying to gray—
Down to the shore, where the Pacific, placid,
Misted and massive, shines with the same milk-blue
That you, if you should turn again and walk
Out to the sunlit balcony, might view.
Seeing the same sea, I, who love, see you.

THE POOL

Rise to the surface, flex and spin and dart
Out of the water, in again, your leap
For the dragonfly that hums above defeated;
If it is caught, you fall with it again
Into the rippled morass of confusion,
Your perfect aim not to be so sustained,
For you are quick or slow beyond control.

Mirroring mountains, dark facsimile
Of yellow pine and blue-scarred granite face,
Your pool suddenly rises with spring rains
And surface melt from ancient snow deposits
Beneath the drift of seasons; or it drops,
In autumn, seeping down through stony gulches
That dry and shine amid the lifting willows.

Within this change you move, minutely felt
By air and water; and the dragonflies
Are real, are food reducible to fish;
And no leap takes you from these waters until
One day the brittle fly is cast and you,
Leaping and drawn at once, are pulled beyond
The flexions and reprisals of the pool.

SUBJECTIVITY

I measure years by days and days by hours
But in the elastic hour of calculation
I leave immeasurable the instrument.
In my delineations watches bend,
The slow distortion of amorphousness,
And now the bullet's flight may be the moth's
When simultaneously I ride with both.
No frozen age, no night perpetual
On Georgian steppes and canyons of the west,
When a dead moon reflects a dying sun,
Turning to the unheard refrains of time,
Is longer, darker, than the eyelid's rest,
The veil of flesh before oblivion.

RED-TAILED HAWK
For Kenneth Fields

Your hawk today floated the loft of air
That lifts each morning from the valley floor.
Dark idler, predator of mice and hare
And greater vermin, as I watched him soar

Out of my sight, taking a certain path,
Knowing from ancient blood, instinctive might,
How to survive beyond the present drift,
He seemed to shift from nothingness toward flight.

Yet it was real, the warm column of air—
Like being, unrecorded, always there.

Nature Note: The California Poison Oak

Dry summers flaw the leaf to a rose flame,
Where, as a vine, it seems to flicker higher
Than live-oaks it consumes, or where it leaps
As a free-standing shrub or tree—ablaze
In wild-oat hayfields. Yet, with winter come,
The stems shrink back and almost disappear
In sinuous tangles, while a few white drupes
That look like snowberries hang to trick the eyes.

Nothing will warn but old experience
The ignorant damp hand that comes to dig
In winter rain the dormant trillium:
Seeking to bring a wild spring beauty home
It finds, as parasitic as a drug,
Pain stinging flesh that brushed the stems but once.

ELEGY AT BEAVERHEAD COUNTY, MONTANA

"Oro y plata"

My father fished here summers, scaled and cleaned
His catch by the gray weathered fence that dips
Into the river. Thin as a pine, he leaned
Again to rinse the knife in chilling rips.

The river is Missouri's western source,
So clear and shallow even stones and sand
Under that sun seem golden in its course.
Men came for gold and, failing, took the land.

Sons of unsettled men sometimes remained
To change the land through labor and design.
He left, rejecting when he might have gained,
But only found another ore to mine.

His quiet lapsed to taciturnity,
Slow anger to hard answers in a glance;
Music alone and its brief gaiety,
His father's gift, remained from circumstance.

For that rich butte in whose deep shaft he died,
Where I first saw, as silver as its earth,
Another stream flow west from the Divide,
Gave to him nothing of its final worth.

POINT LOBOS, 1950

A meadow of wild grass, heather, and sage
Lies here amid the promontory hills
Out of the view of either white-rimmed bay,
Whose indentation marks the coastal sills.
Water that lay below the winds' upheaval
Moves through the turbulence of reef and spray
To calm again, clouding above the cypress.
The scene is fixed within the tranquil day

And is held firm without my mind, while I
Remember a high plain, barren of trees,
A granite-sanded butte immersed in sage,
A pitted hill of copper, manganese,
Silver and quartz, of porphyry and gold,
A gutted hill that poured a copper creek
Steaming into the cold, unburdened air,
Bearing as dross what later men will seek.

It is as if this time were that again,
Found in the scent of sage so perfectly
It is held whole within the mind this once
United to myself and I left free.
For memory that carried too much pain
For men destroyed by earth, then buried there,
Would not appear nor yet be exorcised
But altered sense, as ghosts have altered air.

And as the face, obscure and incomplete,
Which love, deprived, creates when it must change,
That time survived, unknown, in other times

And was perceived in innocence as strange.
Till other change, willed or induced by age,
Delivered feeling from servility,
Revealed and yet assuaged the pain of loss,
Letting the lost appear as it must be.

THE RETURN

Once in September, having crossed the desert,
I came again where I had been a child.
There the high granite range that cleaves the blue
And backs a continent with river sources
Rose above fragile houses and ravines
Sheltering aspens. The dun slopes of sage
And shriveled juniper seemed raw and nude,
As if winter were the permanent condition—
Summer an accident in the long cold.
The children still played in the sandy gulches,
Their mothers called, their fathers still came home
Down rutted roads—their cars the welcome sound
Of dusk—where once my own never returned.
What does one hope to find and why should I
Delight that some things there still wore the look
Of thirty years ago, if not that there
The means of reconcilement lay at hand
As simple as a glance or word, if I
Would have the patience to be still and listen.
Not the rough land, which I can now endure
And love a little, but old voices asked—
The inner dialogue of self with self—
Either a reconcilement or a death.

He was the first to speak: "At your return
Old faith may hold you here in true existence,
Seeing yourself as like yourself at last—
Perception fitting the pattern of your action
As does the final print its negative.
You have been able to come home again,

Leaving the hunt, where hunting you were quarry.
Return is reckoned sweet to him who finds
After his prodigality a portion,
After unfilialness a steadfast father."
She answered, "I have none. That one now silent,
Whose grave I come to walk beside, said nothing,
Living, that I can now remember. He
Hunted these mountains. His father killed the
    coyote,

Wildcat and wolf and elk, trapped bear and beaver,
Up where Missouri starts its yellow flow
In streams diaphanous as air I saw
Gutted red entrails stain their purity;
The startled emptiness of soul where fear
And the deep wilderness seep in to quicken
Malice—the brute's resistance to the brutal.
Near in my blood the memory of famine,
Old-country hunger and humiliation,
Prairie endurance, bone-consuming labor,
The fields and mines, dark streets alive in me.
Their exile is my history; their loss is mine,
Neither to be forgotten nor forgiven."
        He said, "All this is memory and is true,
The child cries in the darkened room where adults
Stumble and cannot find the light. But you
Forget too easily the other strain
That runs in you, the willing immigrant,
That other exile, ready in wit and learning,
Who came to study and teach the moral knowledge
His faith transmitted. Consider why he came."
She answered, "Yet he never came to priesthood.

His eyes failed him. He married, and then dying,
Left a good father's children fatherless,
His faith untaught, for them an emptiness.
Life wastes the things that faith brings into being.
I would be free from fathers, all of them,
Images, substitutes, and real ones, too.
Men are but men, all trying to be fathers,
And falling back to sonship weak with need,
And loving purely not even their own daughters.
I would be like someone who has no gods,
Neither real, imagined, nor the human kind."
And he: "You know, not even the purest skeptic
Lives without his idolatry. Sometimes
That one who seems the freest has the worst—
Himself enshrined, least placable of gods.
Serve, then, the best—the true discerned as truth."
      Then she: "Truth is a varying thing, for man
Still changes his self-image. Having once thought
That we were made in the image of a god,
Or gods like us, now we have taken beasts
For models—mild or violent. Some will have
Our pattern the machines that we have made.
I would be hunter of myself and others.
In such captivity the snare seems sweet,
Even to be destroyed, mirroring seasons.
This need is more than mine; it defines me."

      And he: "The longing not to be prevails,
Powerful and vague whenever what is first
In what is real fails to be first in thought.
You have a certain concept of the real:
Pure nature over against pure nothingness—

The modernists' 'wide water without sound.'
Though nature should endure millennia,
Galaxies rise and spread their arms and fade,
Still one must ask the existential question,
Why anything at all rather than nothing?
Moment by moment I first know I am;
You, hating what you are, hate that you are.
Your concept of the real assumes existence,
And does not face it as mine does. In mine,
The God whose essence is existence grants
Existence momently, then gives himself
Again in drawing you in *caritas*.
Your science tells me only of what is;
Mine deals with that there is a 'what' at all.
Narcissus drowned. Nature need not deceive
Nor drown stout swimmers, able reasoners,
Who think not only outward from the flesh
Nor inward from the mere abstracted mime,
But in and out at once—mind's lightning motion
That knows existence in the existing self—
Concept and percept true to all the fact—
And knows existence given, not of its making.

   "Being as given to every living thing
Is like the light of middle morning sun,
A plenitude adjusted to the eye,
Not darkness nor the radiance of noon,
Too strong for sight. Being is always here;
Nothingness is not, though your mind and will
Conspire to conjure fictions of the void."
She still: "Our minds make all the light there is.
Beyond is only darkness. Darker the way

You Christians take as means to light than death
Itself and the last sleep I shall lie down to,
Grateful for rest."

                    "Darker and viler, yes,"
He answered, "Painful, vile and violent,
Because it is most human. Darker the way
Of that man, taken in faith, than any other,
Because he had most being to undo.
To abnegate the self to find the other,
To give up passion for dispassionate love,
To find, as he, the way to perfect loss
Is an endeavor without glamour, humdrum
As traffic, where the rule is stop and go
On mechanistic orders or be killed;
Yet life seems sweet beyond your expectation
And you obey the lights."

                    "Obey and live,"
She said. "Your way I should obey and die.
All that I call myself would die, if I
Submitted to that rule. I keep my effort
For ends that reason sees, that men can compass,
The quarry always worthy of the hunt,
Lost though the hunter be."

                    Then he, at last:
    "When reason deals with what comes not from
        reason
It posits it too easily as nothing.
Your knowledge suits your will; your will, your
        passion.

Your way, self-circumscribed, ends in the self
And founders there. Mine exiting from loss,
As does an infant from the womb to life,
Integrates its return with its beginning."

HOLY SONNETS

I

I did not see you even when I went
From the long afternoon's forgetfulness
Into a night of knowing the distress
Of questioning your presence and intent.
If you I look for, when my discontent
Is more than tentative unhappiness,
Are not the mere reply of mind in stress,
Be with me casual and concomitant
As gentle breathing in a midnight sleep,
When no one bids the breast to rise and fall.
Be as a quiet fire of which I keep
Enduring warmth in blood the veins recall,
When love, released from too much freedom, tries
The film of cold on hands and lips and eyes.

II

If I had stood waiting for you to come,
Expecting your arrival momently
With bells and horns, the sounding of a drum—
All the mechanic signs of victory—
Of course I had deceived myself, because
I knew that I must travel to the end
Of me, departing thence to that which was
No part of me. While I could still contend
"Perhaps you'll not be there," I still could pause,
Always before the word that you prescribe,
And fail to find you. For, though you, the same
Who waits upon the border, circumscribe
Infinity, denial in me was
Infinity and bore a different name.

ERROR PURSUED

I

Guilt unavowed is guilt in its extreme.
It still accumulates with strict regard
For time and act, although you cannot name
The creditor you owe. And your supreme
Defiance stirs rough gestures that have marred
Your art beyond repair or graceful shame.
Arrogance is a pose disclosing fear
Of law, whose constancy will let you die.
Nor mind nor body is your own to bend
In final alteration; even here,
Where the offending will would still deny
Dependence, know denial too must end.

II

Satan in Eden was "constrain'd
Into a beast."
All of the proud, like him, are pained,
And you not least,
To wear the flesh of which we all are made.

It was a means for him and Christ.
Shrewder than we,
Each knew for what he sacrificed.
Carnality
Destroys when not accepted and allayed.

It is the gift of punishment
That you refuse.
You say you sin without consent
And thus excuse
Self-pity and self-hate—and your despair.

For self is faithless to its end.
Not wife or child
Will fail as badly, nor has friend
As soon beguiled.
It is your way, and you are most aware.

THE ROMANTIC EROS

Your name is Nothing. God without being, sly,
Your forms seem infinite and always lie.
Passion ignores what is to reach for you,
Untouchable, unanswering, untrue.

All that I am not, cannot be, and was
You promise in seducing me, because,
Unreal, you realize yourself in me.
I thought my coldness was your property.

Fled from your country I look back and see
Gray boulders, broken mountains, one high tree,
Infertile, windless, where the black dogs hover,
Self-eaten, not in time or space, but never.

For I now judge what is, be it this or this,
To be a good. Evil is not what is,
But is good's absence, construed as absolute
For passion's paradoxical pursuit.

Careless of what I cannot keep though rare,
My restless hand, no shadow moving there,
Touches what is and lets it go alone,
Both child and friend, loved and unloved-thus known.

Autumn Drought

In memory of Yvor Winters
Stanford University 1976

November brings no rain. Brown stubble blackens.
Torn paper litter, wind-blown with the leaves,
Piles up against dead stems. As traffic slackens,
Nightfall brings fear, and always now one grieves.

Where I once listened, lonely as these young,
But with some hope beyond what I could see
That meaning might be mastered by my tongue,
Anonymous process now claims them and me.

Perhaps the enterprise of mind is vain;
Where hucksters sell opinions, knowledge fails,
Wit pandering to the market, for gross gain,
Corrupted words, false morals, falser tales.

Though one I loved taught here, provoking strife
By speaking truth about the human word,
And died—as few men do—ready for life,
I, teaching in his absence, seem absurd,

Seem almost unremembering, unawake.
And should his poems live—some consolation
To those who knew him and to those who take
His measure by their worth—their celebration

Will not be here, not where the idle gaze,
Touristic, slides past phoenix palms to stare
Where Mount Diablo dominates through haze
The ever-diminishing waters and the glare.

CELEBRATION

Lumen de lumine

For Barbara, Roy, and Christian

Another spring dries in the wild-oat grasses.
The morning wind rises in leaves of rose
And radiant green—the black-oak at our windows—
While ocean fog drifts down the skyline passes.
Before the summer's leaf and its repose
Mowers will pile the white-gold hay in windrows.

In this loved scene being and essence shine;
It is and is itself, like Dante's wheel,
While whole and part, each subatomic spark,
Dependent for existence, undivine,
Disclose the self-existent, first and real.
Light springs from light and not from primal dark.

For you, your Grecian spring may come again.
Some forms of truth descending in the mind
Will seek embodiment, will shape a face,
A concept, or a choice—held to with pain.
And Themis, even, who guides the hours, may find
The infant on your arm outleap her grace.

If he evade the wizard dreamers' chants,
The narcissists of will and of detail,
Through ambuscades of lesser sophists slip,
Inchoatists and devotees of chance,
He may arrive where wisdom might not fail,
Knowing himself, accepting man's sonship.

This is my wish, though it escape my gift:
That he, grown far from you in space and years,
Might be yours still in mind and heart, all ways,
Reflecting then, though all perspectives shift,
The faith that his existence now declares,
And the rare love that your dear presence says.

Visible and Invisible

In touching gently like a golden finger,
The sunlight, falling as a steady shimmer
Through curling fruit leaves, fills the mind with
    hunger
For meaning in the time and light of summer.

Dispersed by myriad surfaces in falling,
Drawn into green and into air dissolving,
Light seems uncaught by sudden sight or feeling.
Remembered, it gives rise to one's believing

Its truth resides in constant speed descending.
The momentary beauty is attendant.
A flicker of the animate responding
Shifts in the mind with time and fades, inconstant.

THREE POEMS FROM MICHELANGELO

1. "L'alma, inquieta e confusa, in sè non trova . . . "

Restless, I find no other cause
Than faults I could not bear to face,
Though not for that hidden from grace—
Immense requirement that grace was.
My Lord, each trial of mine that does
Without your blood brings me no peace.
Have pity on me. These new ways
Are not for me, born to your laws.

2. "Giunto è gia il corso della vita mia . . ."

This is the end of a long drive
As old and treacherous as my car,
And how I happen to be here
I should account for while alive.

Art's subtle tyrannies derive
From fancy's hidden lies, which are,
I now know well, what each must bear,
Against his will, who would survive.

What use are idle thoughts of love
As both my deaths draw near? The end
Of flesh is sure; less sure soul's loss.
When neither paint nor sculpture quiets
My mind, I turn to that one love
Who opened his arms on the cross.

3. "Non può, Signor mio car, la fresca e verde . . ."
To Tommaso Cavalieri

When young, my Lord, we cannot guess
How great the change with age will be—
In tastes and loves, thoughts and desires.

As the soul gains the world seems less,
And death with art does not agree.

What more, then, do you hope from me?

DEGREES OF SHADE

Sic autem se habet omnis creatura ad Deum
sicut aer ad solem illuminantem.

Thomas Aquinas

Our darkness stays, the self-made dark we know,
And I, ever desiring to be right,
Am ever more removed, conceiving not—
As foot can feel the earth and hand, the snow,
And still be unaware— I live in light,
Within yet willfully without your thought.

Your partial absence, as a shade, extends
Upon the brightness that my will obscures.
I am confounded by degrees of shade
And sometimes think the shade's arc reascends
To perfect separation. But I am yours,
Though nothing, if again I am unmade.

I cannot do as some in rage have done,
Who hating love's compulsion love their hate
So much they slay themselves perfecting it.
The course must be endured that was begun
In shade's dominion and empowered so late
To move from out the darkness you permit.

INDECISION

Identity, known or unknown, survives
The lost untempered anguish and the waste.
Its hardness holds, affirming him who grieves.
What he is not and is it says till death.
Then, as a diamond when the chisel cleaves,
It is a perfect whole or only dust.

Unless, against time's claim of absolute,
Spirit should be Christ's flesh, not habitant,
And rest, itself unchanged, in time's estate,
The righteousness of days one may have spent
Learning the surest speech, the oldest act,
Will have but sanctity of precedent.

And while we live we still are free to choose
In his perfected death and resurrection
To see all minor deaths and thereby lose
Delight in change for final absolution.
Or we may wait the death none can refuse
Which will, itself, be in time's disposition.

GOOD FRIDAY

In time a timeless act,
Done once and not again;
For us a constant fact
And paradigm of pain.

Nothingness is our need:
Insatiable the guilt
For which in thought and deed
We break what we have built.

Nothingness draws us down
A vortex of confusion,
Where shape appears to drown,
And being seems delusion.

But being is the given,
From birth to death a grace,
Though some remain unshriven,
Blind in their need's embrace.

And some will never guess
That in the pall we lay,
Symbol of nothingness,
Over the cross this day

Our need is consummated,
Unbeing is undone,
He who was uncreated
Existing where was none.

THE GIFT

I had a gift once that I then refused.
Now, when I take it, though I be accused
Of softness, cant, self-weariness at best,
Of failure, fear, neurosis, and the rest,
Still, I am here and I shall not remove.
I know my need. And this reluctant love,
This little that I have, is something true,
Sign of the unrevealed that lies in you.
Grace is the gift. To take it my concern—
Itself the only possible return.

FOR AN END

Had I not loved,
I had not believed,
And not believing,
Had been deceived.

Had I not loved,
I had not known
Either your being
Or my own.

Had I not loved,
I had not known
That you could love
Both mind and bone.

Had you not loved,
When your decree
Seemed total loss,
You had lost me.

ON THE TWO MARYS IN A FRESCO OF THE CRUCIFIXION

The purer Eve and the impure,
Stand here forever separate.
One love seems all that is secure;
The other, tenuous and late.

One love seems stronger, never crossed,
Maternal passion simplified.
Perhaps it is. The other's cost
In devils mitigates its pride.

On Emily Dickinson

Daimon or angel, in her wrath,
She withdrew wound by wound,
Into her lonely dream of death,
Into one narrow sound.

Ranked spheres on archangelic heights,
Beyond her special glance,
Still sing of where dust ends, and light,
Unending light, begins.

For Edgar Bowers
After Callimachus

I heard that you were dead, Edgar, and wept.
I thought of times at Miramar we watched
The sun go down, the southern stars emerge,
Hearing the long roll and the crash of surf,
While we sat talking, laughing, drinking till dawn.

Your ashes lie now by our western sea,
Quiet as those of Winters and Valéry.

Your poems live, the spirit's breath and seed.
Hades, who would take all, spares them his greed.

MELVILLIANA

1. Moby Dick

I, Ishmael, hunted him, but now no more.
My soul was caught, although he ran before.

2. Bartleby the Scrivener
"I prefer not to."

His gentle preference endures,
In some of us as bitter indignation,
In some as willfulness or whim,
Or new philosophy.

History's strict demand ensures
Survival only of the strict creation:
Our anger's cause exposed in him,
Our longing not to be.

3. Benito Cereno

Knowledge of evil was his only good;
His evil, or whose, he never understood.

4. The Confidence Man

The tongue that carries malice from the heart
May hint plain truth, but hint it with such art
Its victim hears it as ironic jest.
So parodies of truth hide truth the best.

5. Billy Budd

Though slander struck him when he knew no guilt,
His anger made the slander true. Vere saw
His certain death, knowing his certain guilt,
And could not love, though Billy did, the law.

Original Sin

From the beginning life holds death in me.
Twin-born these needs: to be and not to be.

SIERRA NEVADA HIKE

You, Lord, are all my guide. Where I still fail
Is lack of breath: too high, too steep the trail.

EPIGRAMS

Phony now has good fortune and a wife
Who's faithful. Yet he holds you with his tale
Of hardship, broken promises, loves crossed.
Huckster of woe, he plays it to the life
To win your coin of trust, then cry betrayal:
He trades upon the language of the lost.

Janus praised truth. To keep it from abuse
He seldom spoke it. It was too good for use.

Slander accused a woman of assault
Who only meant to sympathize, a fault
He could not bear, for it revealed his need.
Her comfort is she knows her faults, indeed,
For them will answer. When he knows his as well
Let him be candid. But then he would not tell.

Poet admires the young man's poem for this:
"It is your own. All is as you require it."
But subject, tone, and feeling all are his.
I wrote this in his style. He may admire it.

LITERARY THEORIST

Abusing its otherness, its soul and wit,
He rapes the text, claiming its benefit—
And that, inscrutable, it asked for it.

On a Painting by Todd Price of the 16th Michigan Infantry on Little Round Top, July 2, 1863

Waves of assault break on this rocky spur—
Prow of our Ship, driven to this fierce place.
Whom the surge takes and who remains to cheer
God knows. His storm hides even our brother's face.

III
CROSSING THE PEDREGAL

LEMUEL SHAW'S MEDITATION

> "Who's to doom, when the judge himself is dragged to the
>   bar?"
>
>   Melville's Ahab

Boston, January 1861

Through this sad winter as our crisis deepens,
And war so long resisted now seems certain,
When I, more ill than old, have given up
At last the Commonwealth's chief-justiceship,
I have gone back in mind—not reminiscent
But searching—remembering what was said and done
For better or for worse by men like me,
Who, mindful of the welfare of the whole,
Have sought to keep the Union from disaster,
Believing—whether we prove wrong or right—
That its survival is man's dearest hope;
Remembering also what was said and done
By other men, who were, I felt, too partial
To special causes, private moralities.
Yet it is he I most remember now,
My son-in-law, a poet in his soul,
Though our prose age rewards the pleasant tale,
The South Sea narrative, or boy's adventure,
Most volatile of men and yet most earnest,
Who listened, quiet, to my recondite,
Because so rarely spoken, considerations.

Twelve years ago he came and we discussed
What then preoccupied all thinking men,
Which we had touched on only casually
At earlier meetings, discreetly, as men did
Who feared the fear the topic slavery
Aroused and still arouses; though now, long past

The needs of politesse, all speak of war.
Led by some words of mine about the case,
Seven years earlier, of Latimer,
Which was my first concerning a fugitive,
He asked me in his candid, eager way:
"I wonder, sir, how you, having the power,
Knowing the scourge you would return him to,
Could not find means, legal or otherwise,
To let him stay on Massachusetts soil,
A man like others, standing in the sun?"

Quick to respond to his frank earnestness,
I answered by recalling his own youth:
"To see the case as I saw Latimer's,
Posit a legal case that might be drawn
From your experience, your years at sea,
Your time aboard a U.S. Navy ship.
For states, you know, and nations are like ships;
In stress their laws resemble those of ships.
Suppose a British sailor in time of war
During the years the British fought the French,
Was forced—impressed—into the Royal Navy,
And he, though loyal, unresentful, were
Trapped by the malice of a lesser man,
Accused of stirring mutiny; and he
Struck out and killed the man, an officer,

Defensive of his honor—murder not meant.
Say, then, the Captain, caught by circumstance,
Was called to judge, knowing the sailor's aim
Neither rebellious nor homicidal,
But manly in its self-defensive posture,
Seeing the inward honesty and pride
(Sharing, perhaps, that honesty and pride)
Reasoned that he must take the penalty
Which naval law prescribes in time of war,
More needed, even, in time of mutinous
And unpredictable unrest at sea.
Suppose his reasoning was that equity—
The means our human law allows sometimes
For its adjustment to the special case,
Or for appeal to timeless principles,
Granting a precedence to natural law—
Could not apply, when what was here at stake
Was ship and crew, the fleet, perhaps the nation—
Beyond the nation, values that it stood for
Against the French Directory's tyranny.
Suppose he saw, but could not change the case:
Conflict of rights, ancient as human law,
The individual's claim to justice locked
In mortal strife with welfare of the whole.
Evil begets itself and traps the good,
Forcing the lesser's sacrifice to greater.

     "So I, aware of our ship's tenuous union,
Our federation on one fragile keel
(Because still weak the bonds between the states—
Weak through injustice to the African)
Yet loyal to the Union's hopes, its vision,

Its possibilities, in time, for all,
I reasoned (and all we have against our fate
Is reason's ranging gaze) that my response
Must take account of welfare of the whole,
Holding in mind its destined hope for all,
For him, his children, and his children's children—
Must for the Union's sake deny his plea.
For if the Union fail because the South
Could not depend on Northern loyalty
To oaths and laws, made at our sacred union,
Then there fail also all our hopes for freedom—
Freedom, I mean, for all, when time might alter
The Europeans' fear of Africans.
And if the Union fail, the South might forge
An empire monstrous in potential evil,
Founded on systematic degradation,
Bordering us, a constant source of friction
Beyond our power to modify or change.
Among these evils I sought out the least,
Keeping my oath to Constitutional law,
Flawed as it is, hoping to alter it."

Thus I gave my account to Melville, quiet,
The cases not the same but judged on issues
That were alike—the Captain's and my own:
Both conflicts where the law, made to preserve
A nation's welfare—at the last ditch its life—
Clashes with rights founded in natural law,
The law some hold divine in origin,
And some our reason's highest discovery.
So I, recalling how I thought and felt
When I said Latimer must be remanded,

Tried to explain the reasons for my judgment
And hoped he comprehended my position.
Perhaps he understood, perhaps not so.
But he, a storyteller, would remember,
I'm sure, the case, and he, a thoughtful man,
Would look at all sides of the question posed,
Then probe with his quick sensibility
What I, living and acting tragedy,
Cannot articulate but only feel.

Then he that day, scanning the current news,
The problems posed by California's statehood
Unbalancing the Senate's equipoise,
And by the opening of the territories,
Touched on the danger posed to our frail Union
By one-idea'd men on either side:
Whether the Abolitionists' extreme,
Who see the system as "Diabolus"
(Their phrase), the war on Satan their salvation
And its destruction their Millennium—
Enthusiasts, in whose noble-seeming fervor
Both he and I felt our hearts share, indeed,
While our minds saw impossibility
Of implementation of the good we dream of.
The other side, a disease, a moral cancer
Breeding on fear and greed, inherited,
Erected to a systematic code—
Mind's effort to enthrone a mindless fear.
And he, mulling the while how Fate might go,
Narrated me a legend he had heard
Or read, perhaps, at sea, though he, as always,
Shaped, colored, and embellished it with skill

Beyond my dry and ponderous style yet I,
As I recall, saw nestled in its flesh
The bone and sinew of enduring questions,
Drew from its shell the rich and nutty kernel—
The tragic point whereon his story turned—
Choice, always choice, amid a maze of errors:
Our necessary judgment among evils,
Its cost, sometimes, more than our lives are worth.

       He told this story, while I saw a case:
There was a whaler, captained by a man,
Who in his unchecked willfulness resembled
Valentine Pease, captain of his *Acushnet*—
Unbalanced then, or near it, as he told me.
This whaling captain's story was a legend,
One of the tales the South Seas' fisheries
Abounded in of monstrous creatures, real
Themselves, but giving birth in sailors' minds,
Prone to the superstitions of their calling,
To narratives embellished by their fictions.
This man was crippled by a sperm whale's jaw,
And, swearing vengeance, maddened to despair,
Saw absolute evil incarnate in the beast,
Swore that his vindication by its destruction
Would be real justice, when nor God nor man
Could give it him. With this strong motive's power,
And offering gold to those who missed the symbol,
He terrorized his mates and crew, drew them,
With him, into an oceanic search,
A chase, a last encounter on the Line,
Where, when the whale's head struck and breached
    their ship,

Both ship and captain, mates and crew all
    foundered.

        To him this plot seemed one where the
    sublime,
Which his romantic readers sought, might rise
From genuine terror, superstitious dread,
Grounded in real sea-life, while his own aim—
A classical one, to show how human choice,
Intricate with self-generated fault,
Brings on a fatal, violent, conclusion—
Was met in the mad captain's self-willed thrust
To carry out this cause at any risk
To those for whom he was responsible.
This story seemed almost to haunt his mind.
Listening to Melville, I, too, felt its power
Beyond the ordinary. And, then, he added,
Expanding on it, that the captain seemed
Bewitched by evil, like those deluded victims
Of witchcraft in West-African belief
To whom their fear of Obi power brings death;
Or like those other vexed men closer home,
The Salem Puritans, Mather and Sewall,
Who saw the Devil incarnate, evil itself
Embodied in their fellowmen, and hanged them—
Later, recanting, confessed they were deluded.

        I, then, responding from my side, replied
That, likewise, I felt I had been the victim
Of righteous-seeming men of good intent,
Possessed by one idea, that slavery
Was demonism incarnate, "sum of all evils,"

70

As Wesley called it, and I, bound by my oath,
My reasoning on my higher duty to freedom,
Who made the choice to send back Latimer,
I was regarded as the devotee,
In their rapt superstitious minds, of Satan,
Or Pilate giving over Christ to death.
My mild complaint he took in political sense.

Then I, returning to his legend, told him
I saw in it, with my dry mind, a case:
The posthumous trial of a whaling captain
For negligence—his ship, crew, cargo lost,
But for one sailor, who survived as witness
(For we would need that one to tell the tale).
The issues drawn, I made analogy
Again of ship with nation, and of its captain
With men who were elected or appointed,
Sworn to our Constitution and the Union,
Who might, citing their call to higher law,
Act and call others into potent action
To eradicate forthwith, at any cost,
The beast that sullies all our days and nights,
Thus risking all, the welfare of the whole,
Our mingled crew of multi-origined persons
To satisfy their one-idea'd passion—
Moral, indeed, aiming at good, but wrong
In practice, loosing, through their benevolence,
Malevolence beyond imagination.

Moreover, some men's virtue seemed,
    I thought,
Suspicious in its roots, its motivation.

I meant such men as ice-proud Emerson,
Who said once that a thousand Negroes captive
Meant to him nothing, but that slavery
Demeaned the white man's moral qualities,
Men like himself in birth and education.
Humane? Benevolent? Or misanthropic?
Such literary men, not called to judge,
Or act, or speak in public life, the arena,
Profit from freedoms I've not had. "But you,"
I said to Melville, "my more than son, have lived
Where lives depend upon the instant judgment
Of one who may or may not know his duty."

       Thus I went on—so long ago, it seems—
"If this, our Union, which is for all of us
The past, our present, and the future of men,
Were swayed by leadership of one who set
Private concerns above our state's survival,
I fear the beast would win, would bring us down—
Ship, crew, and cargo. Such a man would risk,
Like the demented captain in your story,
His ship—our all—against his duty, sworn,
For private satisfaction, his salvation,
Found, as he thinks, in ending this one evil,
Though evil is endemic to the end,
And our hope but to modify its power."

       Then I recalled a speech made years ago,
A strong lyceum speech in Illinois
By a young Western lawyer, a Whig like me,
That made my point exactly: the risk we ran
In that mob-ridden time, prelude to this,

That some mad, towering genius, seeking glory,
Through antislavery or its opposite,
Might overturn our laws, for personal fame,
Might break the Union to enhance his name.
The lawyer urged obedience to law
Till laws, if bad, as slavery's code, be changed.

      I said all this, mulling and ruminating
As only in his company I could;
And he responded in his earnest way
That he, too, saw the possibility
Of turning sea-experiences unused
To more ambitious ends than anecdote—
Might find a way to join the rich detail,
Remembered, of his whaling life to plot
And characters symbolic of our crisis;
Might even share my legalistic vision
To shape his story as a legal case
In which the judgment made by judge or jury
Would be dependent mainly on the witness—
The sole survivor of the tragic wreck—
Whose voice might be the listener's guide to
    Judgment,
Albeit one sympathetic to his captain,
Feeling his hate for what the beast was sign of,
Sharing his love for justice our world lacks.
The sailor might be advocate as well,
Defend the captain's choice through his own words,
Show his inducement, provocations, losses,
The great nobility of his great cause;
Yet tell the rational mate's objection, too,
Display the weakness of the other mates,

Their mediocrity and soullessness.
"But he, the sailor-witness," Melville went on,
"Would judge and help the listening audience judge
Where woe for sins was wisdom and where madness.
An injured man himself, who learned at sea
Humility before the powers of evil
In man and nature, he might be," he said,
"A nearly perfect witness to tragedy,
Like the old choruses in Sophocles
And Aeschylus I have been reading lately."

I answered that he might in his account
Show both the sides, or many sides, of this,
The most vexed problem in our politics:
That high and moral aims may lead to ends
Worse than the evil sought to be dispelled.
I saw how this kindled his ardent nature—
Eager to sympathize with injured men,
Quick to perceive an evil where it is,
But likewise quick in his intelligence
To see the consequences of a choice,
To guess the tragic costs in human life.

Well, that seems long ago, though not so
    long,
Really, in years. Yet he in these twelve years
Has aged, I feel, till he seems old as I,
With all my court work, business, social life.
His tragic romance, written to some faint praise
But little understanding of its depth,
Gave him much grief. His latest book displays
A withering satire on our politicians,

On selfish men who prey on confidence,
Like demons in exploitative subterfuge—
Satire that's worthy of my favorite Hogarth,
More finely grained in verbal wit than Swift.
He seems, because his eyes and mind disclose
A poet's heart, ravaged by his perceptions.
I call him poet, now, for only as poet
Will he have power to speak of what is coming,
That which I know I'll not survive to see:
The tragedy that his wild legend fixed
In emblematic form, as prophecy,
Is now unfolding as the states secede.
The social system that outraged our hearts,
With which we compromised to save the Union
That it, in turn, might save them from themselves,
Seems now in charge as, singly, its white victims
Withdraw from union with their greater good,
And we, their brothers, must treat them as traitors.

       The springs of this event are numberless.
We both have watched with grief the gathering
    storm.
Now he will stay to see it out, to tell
In verse, not fiction, how the battles go.
And I, now that I have no duty, am free
To yield to what my heart has always held—
Released by their secession from our bond
To give them back their slaves and keep them safe—
Possibly free, even, through violence
To see the slaves freed. That may yet be seen.
If this young lawyer—no one-idea'd Ahab
Nor coward Starbuck he—can find his way

75

As President, during the coming conflict
To use his war powers, citing the Union's need
In mortal danger, for black-soldier power,
Ending the nightmare slavery has been,
Though he'll not change our human nature's evil,
He might permit a lessening of the wrong,
A small increase of right.

                  Now, argument,
Reason's persuasive eloquence, gives way
To grand unreason. Now it begins
That will be settled only by sword and gun.

MELVILLE'S LETTER TO WILLIAM CLARK RUSSELL

victrix causa deis placuit sed victa Catoni
—Lucan, *Bellum Civile* I, 128

For G. E. L.

New York City, 1888

You ask me, Russell, why we fought and why,
These long years after Appomattox, we
Conceal, as if it were an unhealed wound,
The motives, costs, and choices from ourselves;
Why we call it the "late unpleasantness,"
Shielding from foreign eyes our damaged past.
I thought once that I knew. When in the months
That followed Lee's surrender I composed
My battle poems, praising the dead and living,
The gallant captains and their men, naming
The fields and rivers where they gave their blood
For principles that reason could not weigh
While funeral lights still flared, I did not see,
Though I saw more than most, that a just cause
May not be always visible to all,
That, like Antigone's appeal to laws
Unwritten and unchanging, some true claims
Must reach beyond human authority.

Then I saw only that the Southrons cherished
Their hearths and altars, feudal fidelity
To home and soil, as Hawthorne wrote, when he,
Visiting occupied Virginia, saw

77

Women and men, by the anomaly
Of two allegiances perplexed, choosing
The claim that lies nearest the human heart
And not an airy mode of written law
That had no symbol but a flag—their choice
Like Colonel Lee's, who would not raise his sword
Against his kin, his home, his children. I knew
(Though honor answered honor there, when
    Gordon
Dipped his worn sword to Chamberlain's salute)
That the muskets stacked on Appomattox road
Had fired four years, by ford and farm, to curb
The newly wakened Northern will to rule—
An imperial goal beyond the Founders' pact
Of federated States, yet one that would,
So I believed, establish Right through might.
Those ends, at least, I saw in Sixty-Five
And wrote of them. I think I see more since:
The bond once cut with a thoroughgoing knife,
The cords might not retie.

                            You ask of Hawthorne:
I think he died of sorrow for the War,
Feeling in his own flesh their pain and sickness,
Reading the bulletins' rain-washed lists of killed,
Wounded, and captured, missing, drowned—the
    names.
So many were the deaths he could not bear them,
Felt, as he said, unnecessary, while
The Eden-like mild landscape of our youth
Vanished, and Massachusetts boys he knew—
Sons of his friends, or nephews, or young brothers—

Played out the tragedy we had foreseen
But had not guessed the actors nor the places:
At Ball's Bluff, where the bullets sprayed the
    Potomac
Like a rain-shower; at Glendale; at Antietam,
When the red sun seemed almost to go backward,
So slow the day, so endless seemed the firing;
The heights at Fredericksburg, where Cobb's men
    saw
Our blue ranks melt like snow, and the living piled
The frozen dead as breastworks; in Stonewall's
    storms
At Manassas and Chancellorsville; in the three great
    acts
At Gettysburg. Boys in the wild wind fell
Like autumn leaves in a New England gale,
Or lay in swathes, blue as a Cape Cod pond,
Their fresh young flesh scythed down with ripened
    wheat
Or plucked unripe in orchards, berry patches,
Their bodies, under dying horses' hooves,
Crushed like the late June clover their feet crushed
Hastening to Gettysburg.

       Nor did he live
To hear how blood pooled in the Crater's clay,
Nor how young Lowell died, whom I knew well,
Struck—a sharpshooter's mark—at Cedar Creek
In Sixty-Four, careful as Sidney was,
Dying, that others, who might live, were tended.
For Hawthorne knew his people were the cause
(Part of the cause, for no one cause was all),

Their too profound and savage lust for God
Grown to a pure unchristian hate for evil—
The bosom serpent of the Puritan—
When they found God would always lie beyond
    them.
And, too, he felt accomplice in the sin:
Early New England's profit in slave traffic.

     I have lived on, a hardier, coarser type,
To try to pierce the tangle of decisions
That seemed in Sixty-One enforced by Fate—
Even to hypothesize alternatives,
As fireside warriors do old battle scenes.
I feel as if I might have one tale more,
A naval one (as you might guess), wherein
Dilemmas posed suddenly shape hard choices,
Simple beyond belief in their collision,
Injurious beyond our tears in their effects;
A tale that might show more: how men transcend
Themselves (if that be not too stale a word)
And, sacrificing this world's justice, die
Trusting their judgment at the Last Assizes.
Such I may yet attempt, if my health holds.

     My wife's dear parent (my friend till he died),
Judge Lemuel Shaw, once, long before the War,
Told me an anecdote of naval lore,
Using it, then, to illustrate the hard
And costly choice he had to make in court,
Remanding to the South a fugitive,
Where either choice was evil—duties obliged
By differing laws: one, manmade national law,

The other, natural or divine, deemed higher.
His story's time was the Great Mutiny
In Ninety-Seven, the era you know well,
For you narrate in your fine life of Nelson
Your fleet's unrest at Spithead and the Nore,
When his bold mien restored its discipline.
Shaw's tale was of a frigate's captain then
And a young sailor, who had been impressed,
Both trapped by Fate or by inscrutable malice,
One made the other's executioner
When called to judge between conflicting duties
To national safety or to natural justice,
Which claims for each of us a natural right
To judgment by our motives, not our deed.

Shaw's tale turned on a clash of types of law
(A conflict still bedeviling human wit)
Like that I see was ours in our Rebellion,
Which, smoldering, burst in Sixty-One in flames.
For in the tale a sly ambitious man,
Envying the sailor for his inborn virtues,
Conspires to slander him as mutinous.
In confrontation in the captain's cabin,
The boy, tongue-tied, cannot defend his honor,
Strikes out and kills by chance the officer.
The captain, sure of his duty to the King
(Your empire's symbol), to his ship and men,
Believes in time of unrest far at sea
Even the appearance of lax discipline
Is dangerous. He calls a drumhead court,
Brief in examination of the facts,
And rules that written law, stringently made

For safety of the ship, has claims higher
Than natural justice, which would plead for him
Honorable intent and self-defense,
Despite appearances and accident.
The boy is hanged for killing the officer,
And in the press, blamed for planned mutiny.

The ship sails on in its imperial course,
As ours did after Appomattox's close.
And our official record? Rebellion quelled,
Traitors and miscreants penalized by death,
Our voices raised to cry their shame for decades,
And Right through might, as I said then, made Law.
The issue left unsettled by our Founders—
Whether the Nation or the States were sovereign—
Was settled by the sword. Grant won that case.
Yet, I could not forbear acknowledging
That had preponderance of men and arms
Lain on their side, on us had fallen the stain,
Ignoble, of treason—ours called the Rebel cause.
Your poet John Harrington's wit seems to the point:
"Treason doth never prosper. What's the reason?
Why, if it prosper, none dare call it treason."

For history's texts have inside narratives,
Intricate threads that need to be unraveled.
You know that long before our war were decades
Loud with reciprocal denunciation,
The rant of politicians on both sides,
Tainting the press, pulpit, and legislature
(As when Brooks caned Charles Sumner in the
Senate),

But bitterest the North's anathemas
And slanders, which dishonored honorable men,
Who, goaded, struck impetuously out at Sumter,
As a man given the lie will strike his foe,
As the boy, wordless, struck at his accuser,
While innocent, yet plainly broke the law
And, beyond passion, bravely paid for it.

So, in their payment for that lightning blow,
Fell the South's flower of sons: Ashby and Pelham;
Johnston at Shiloh, with boys from piney woods
And placid bayous; Stonewall, Stuart, and Hill,
"Gone too far forward ever to return";
The skilled in deeds of Mars with novices,
Known with the unknown; Armistead with his
    Virginians,
Garnett with his, and boys from Carolina,
Tennessee, Mississippi, Alabama,
Boldly assaulting, all downed in one fierce
And consecrated charge at Gettysburg;
Cleburne and Gist, new blood with old commingled,
Forfeited in the smoky dusk at Franklin;
Ramseur and Rodes in the devastated Valley;
The Pegram brothers at Hatcher's Run and Five
    Forks,
In the unmatched days along the Appomattox.

So ours paid, too. For from that opening
    blow
And from our Captain's instantly willed decision
That, under threat, the Union would use force
Followed all the rest. Not otherwise, he judged,

Could he decide, given his duty to law
(As he conceived it), to the Constitution,
Our paper pact, a scant seven decades old,
Yet written law, wherein he might construe
A sovereign nation with power to put down States,
Whose claims to sovereignty he disallowed,
Whose right to revolution (the same our fathers
Cited against your King in Seventy-Six)
Lincoln did not deny but disallowed,
Because they had no reason, in his eyes.
Nor could he look to motives, only the deed,
Rebellion plain in act most evident
To him, to us—to me.

                              Yet now I see
More to it, seeing in retrospect how we—
All of us—shared conspiratorial myths,
Our fears engendered by our ignorance—
Even the wisest. Each of us saw the other
As Satan, citing your Milton, saw himself
As archangelic Michael in God's war,
Ennobling thus his cause, but demonizing
The other. In half-light shadows distend to shade.
Each had, like you in your religious quarrels,
A Titus Oates to point the finger of hate,
To blacken names with righteous-seeming wrath.
Conscience in such is lawyer to the will;
They use their reason for irrational ends,
Envying the good.

And there were other motives,
Some hidden then, though now they've borne their
    fruit:
Parties in power identify that power,
And seldom justly, with the nation's good.
The wicked man may always use the good
Unless the good acquire the serpent's wisdom,
Unless he take, though good, saturnine views.
Confidence men then sat (and still they sit)
In our high councils, in our public forums
Citing benevolent ends through unjust means.
Twice in the Wilderness brother sought brother's
    blood,
Believing he served a holier law than self,
The same God's will, while far behind the firing
In capitols and press-rooms lesser men
For worldly ends shaped death. Is it so always?

    Sitting alone, now, free from the Custom
    House,
I read the soldiers' memoirs, letters, journals:
Battles and leaders living still in print,
The individual dramas by the actors.
The tone of many scarcely veils their grief,
Sorrow uncomforted for comrades dead.
Some grew in faith through battle, stronger for stress,
Purer for seeing depths of impurity,
While some seem flowers that bloomed only in
    death,
Their Lord's death modeling theirs. His excellent
    word
The source of their assent, His sacrifice

Gives meaning when invoked on either side,
For cause or country, mankind or kin, or self.
Their prayers make meaningful their felt intent,
And Socrates died for a just intent.
They felt their immortality beyond
The fame we try to give them with our words.

      Your heart, my English friend, can feel for
  both,
As I, never a partisan, feel too.
Some in the North have taken to their hearts
The Union dead as if they were the whole—
"Part of our lives' unalterable good,"
As Harvard's Lowell wrote in his great ode,
And yet he had no word for their sure good,
Who died for deeper cause with less to win,
Perhaps a nation and perhaps their homes,
But only sure their honor. How, I ask now,
Without their dead acknowledged in our temples
(As you honor your rebels in your Abbey)
Can we become one people? When I read how
Lee's men, advancing footsore, felt that day,
Fording the brown Potomac, rifles lifted
And glinting in the hazed September sun,
Singing to Maryland to come and join them,
I'm like the Yankee girl, who, seeing Lee,
Said ruefully, "I wish that he were ours."
Many have wished it.

      You will remember, perhaps,
In my long poem dramatizing Lee
As spokesman for the South before the Senate,

86

I pled, with his imagined eloquence,
For reconcilement, magnanimity;
And, in another, argued for charity,
As Grant showed Lee, which Lincoln meant to show,
Which truest soldiers felt for former foes,
Some of them men who fought and suffered most,
Like Francis Bartlett, my "college colonel," who,
Wounded three times, and captured, weak with
      disease,
At the war's close became a friend to the South.
Such great-souled virtue asks not for repentance
Where no sin was committed, no guilt felt,
But offers a tested hand to tested valor,
Welcoming him to the fellowship of manhood.
Not less, the Massachusetts men young Shaw
Led to a sandy grave below Fort Wagner
Have not received their Southern tears. All should,
Tempered in one indifferent fire, be honored,
For the same innocence and valor moved them.
Would it might be!

                    So, thus, dear Russell, you have
My troubled answer to your thoughtful question;
For the wound bleeds yet in my soul, divided
And suffering yet with them in spirit, but not,
Like them, endowed with holy faith. If I,
Remembering, honoring, suffering as I do,
See only a worldly end as their intention,
Share our time's judgment of the Right made Law,
And its opinion that the Wrong put down
Validated all the blood, and fire, and hate,
Justified, too, the wrong we did our brothers,

Then I could not be true to those who lost,
To whose faith, I without faith, must return,
And in my meditations speak their names.

ALIKE AND YET UNLIKE: GENERAL RICHARD TAYLOR WRITES TO HENRY ADAMS

For C. Q. D.

Washington, D.C., January 1879

We spoke last evening of your work and
  mine,
Of your first novel, of my little essay,
A venture into history, remote
Seemingly, and yet near my heart these days
When none remember what we were, or what
We might have been, had the war never come.
Your manuscript held me from sleep all night,
For it seemed hardly fiction but the truth
About a generation without honor.
And yet I wonder that you do not see
That the corruption you so well depict
Follows as night the day the venal motives
That fired and drove the engine of the war,
The railroads, mills, the arms and armament.
You set the thing in motion with your cause.
It consumed us and now consumes your best.
Even Grant, who acted with Old Army honor
At Appomattox, now has stained his name.
You show him as a simple-minded fool
And show the Union, for which your noblest died,
The foul and rotten Vanity Fair it is.
It's well they are not here to see or know
The end of all their sacrifice, that rabble
Like these rule a democracy of thieves.
Better the quiet grave and unsullied fame!

My illness will excuse, I hope, my anger.
Reading your work, sensing your misery,
I like to think of how it might have been.
You, child of diplomats, skillful with suave words,
And I, of soldiers and the sword, together,
We might have lived, God willing, a happier story.
And I dream, too, without the war, I might
Have been something of an historian,
Had I had quiet hours with documents
To trace out to their hearts our Southern men
As I have Mason, and you, Gallatin.
My little sketch remains, at least, to show
How much we are alike and yet unlike.
With peace we might have built a true republic.

But you did not trust us, did not trust me.
I knew that when, as a boy, I paced the streets
Of wintry Cambridge and heard the cultured sneer
That my soft Southern speech evoked. I read
Your Puritans' serpent-tongued anathemas
And chose the warmer voices of New Haven,
Though it no haven for a Southern boy.
Though seldom with my father after my childhood,
Even then I had, bred in my bones and sinews,
Ancestral habit of battle, my father's gift,
Latent the while I studied it in books.

Last night when you lamented that your
    schooling
Failed to engage your life, it came to me,
Afterward, that you missed the best of schools,
The one your friends all chose in Sixty-One—

Nick Anderson, Ben Crowninshield, your brother,
Your Southern friends, Jim May, and Julius Alston,
And Rooney Lee. In war they learned a truth
Fitted for life because it was of death,
A comradeship at once sublime and useful:
Arm touching arm, bayonets ranked in rows,
Only the thin gray wool, or blue, as armor
Between their frail flesh and the iron hail.
You never heard the shell nor felt the ground's
Motion under the iron cannon's blow,
Nor sensed the hornet's hum about your ears,
Nor forced your trembling horse into the volley,
Nor, like young Alston, tasted dirt and sand,
Blinding your eyes for hours behind your guns.
The wonder of it still catches my breath
When I recall it!

   Your friends learned how to die, surely a
  lesson
Most valuable for life. At least a lesson
That those who lived discovered was a true one.
And I, I believe, learned one more precious thing:
The war's meaning was not its politics,
Was not the secular state, nor mystical Union,
Was not the liberation of a people,
Which would have come as they rose up and
  claimed it;
Not its intention ever nor its results.
It was their confrontation with the timeless.
Before, they had been sleeping, or time-driven,
But then were wakened, ready for timeless effort.

My little history is part of theirs.
May I tell you at least some part of it?
Cutting into the game, staking my life,
My fortune, my children's future, knowing our
     chance
Of winning slight, unable to refuse,
I led my novice regiment to join
Johnston and Beauregard at First Manassas.
Thereafter Davis gave me, kindly as always,
And trusting, my cosmopolitan brigade—
New Orleans Irish, stout and turbulent,
Gentle and gay Acadians from the Tèche,
Some gallant planters' sons from river farms,
And Rob Wheat's Tigers, wharf rats from the levees.
With these a little disciplined, I joined
Jackson and his small army in the Valley.

There, at Front Royal, I saw his star first
     blaze,
Like Sirius, and for my men's small part
Won an approving glance from him, long treasured.
At Winchester one sparkling day in May
We harried Banks back to the Potomac fords.
For this engagement Jackson shook my hand.
But, most of all, my education came
At Port Republic, where at the embattled Coaling
My men with bayonets, muskets clubbed—even
     ramrods—
Set their backs to the mountain to die hard.
Counter-attacking, reinforced, they made
A fourth and final rush and seized the guns,
Turned them, and fired on Shields's retreating men.

In this my Tigers, riffraff of New Orleans,
Men I had tamed our first days in Virginia
By salutary executions, found
That they could fight better than planters' sons,
Than clerks and college boys, and loved me for it.

You asked last night the story of Jackson's
    death.
I spoke once with a Captain Smith, his aide,
Who rode to him the night that he was wounded,
Remaining with him till he died. Smith told me
That nights before the battle the moon looked down,
Lighting the winding Rappahannock's flow,
On rested soldiers, polished guns, fresh earthworks,
Log breastworks, stacked arms, pickets, and
    batteries,
All watchful of the river, the hostile north,
And the vague Wilderness, unfamiliar ground.
At Lee's command they moved. At Jackson's order
All Saturday his silent column wound
Through sassafras, hazel, thickets of pine and oak,
Into ravines and out, waded a run
Where partridge and foolish rabbits sprang from
    cover.
They heard the distant muttering of Lee's guns,
Looked through short vistas cut by blackened
    shadows,
Moving in silent column through the shade,
The men's bare feet slapping the soft dry soil,
Leaving faint prints dashed out by hoofs and
    caissons.
"Press on," he urged them.

Hour after hour they marched
On narrow paths that only farm boys knew,
And came at last onto the old stone road
That led to Chancellorsville, where Hooker slept.
Between them rested and idled Howard's Corps.
Rodes, Colston, and Hill set lines across the road.
At five Rodes signaled his readiness, and Jackson's
Low, gentle voice said, "You may go forward, then."
As they advanced, utterly unsuspected,
The dropping fire of skirmishers then turned
Into the roar of musketry. Bewildered,
The Yankees fled like sheep when the wolf comes
    down.
I should like very much to have been there,
Although in battle we seldom had the leisure
To contemplate sublime effects. And the woods
Concealed the suddenness, masked the terrible
    sound,
The speed and magnitude of Jackson's lines.

                                    The
forward movement crested quickly. With night
The full-moon's light upon the woods lured Jackson
To push on to the river fords, to strike
By night the enemy's rear, cut off retreat,
And fall on him at dawn, crushing his corps
Between his own divisions and those of Lee—
With one triumphant blow win peace for us.
But in the nervous darkness, shadowy confusion,
Jackson rode too far forward. His unwarned men
Fired blindly at the sound of hoofs and struck him,
His staff scattered and fallen in the dark,

Where hoofbeats on the old stone road struck fire.
When Smith arrived, he said, his troubled heart
Most failed him when he saw impetuous Hill,
Whom Jackson had arrested for some fault
And then released for battle, kneel by his chief
To cradle his bleeding head. He saw, faintly,
His rigid face, pale now and deeply scratched,
And blood, so common, uncommon on his face.
Smith cut his sleeve and staunched the shattered arm
With his own kerchief, then helped carry him.

       It was a night that seemed to some of us
To sum up all our losses. Our good man,
Our great man, downed by his own soldiers' fire.
God's humor seems sardonic as my own.
Yet Smith, a minister, saw Christ's agony
In Jackson's wounding in the Wilderness:
His two hands pierced by balls, the shattered arm,
The lacerated face, the falls from the litter,
His pain-wracked wagon journey to the rear,
And then to Guiney's Station, where while all
The South, and I, too, prayed for him, his slow
Descent to death fulfilled a timeless pattern,
Bound all again in the mystery of death
Our education had prepared us for.
We all learned that who heard the hum of minnies
Amid pine branches and the cry of shells.
Your friend, the lawyer Holmes, knows it, for he
Speaks well of hearts touched in their youth with fire.
It is a fire death kindles in the heart,
Like a faithful servant to warm us for eternity.

Because his virtue verified their cause
Jackson's men loved him and believed that God
Was with them when he led, but even more
Because he won. Yet I saw in his eyes,
Once only, an ambition flash that was
Boundless as Cromwell's and as merciless,
Was all-absorbing. He loathed it in himself,
Certainly feared it, but could not escape.
It was himself, his flesh. Yet still he struggled
In constant earnest prayer, as with Apollyon
Engaged in ceaseless combat. Like Christian's, too,
His journey to the River. Still, in the Valley
He played us all like chessmen, secretly,
Utterly obedient to the will of Mars,
As a commander should. I learned of war
From him as from no other but my father—
My father, Jackson, and books. I had done better,
Perhaps, to learn from Lee, for then I might,
After our rout of Banks at Mansfield's fight,
Have curbed my anger and have had my way
With Kirby Smith, and been sent men enough
To shatter Banks and capture Porter's gunboats.
With them, we might have opened the great river
And made our jewel, New Orleans, ours again.
Forgive me if I dream now at my desk.

So what remains? Only to tell you this
About myself and you and all of us:
The God that we love you think you do not,
And yet through us you will believe in Him.
Our loss already claims part of your soul
As well as ours, because it is your history.

You say you don't know who you are, cannot
Trace Washington from the "sum of iniquity,"
Nor ever will till you see slavery
Was not that sum, was not the demon shape
Your wizards cast it as to fire your hate.
Nor were we demons. Your novel tells me you
Already sense that, for your Madeleine
Will marry Carrington, even, perhaps, be happy.

       And what will they recall of us? I think,
When my storm-cradled nation has become
A hidden country of the heart for sons,
Though not for my dear boys, who died too young,
They will remember, surely, moments and men—
Moments when men were more than men, were
    touched
By truth, by love beyond themselves, by honor
Having little to do with secular law.
That which the Greeks called gods and Christians
       God Drew them, sustained them, and when
    necessary
Received them to Himself. Earth holds their dust.
The God your skeptic habit denigrates,
The living God, spoke to them in the Word
They read by smoky firelight or by candles
Socketed in their upturned bayonets,
And then in battle heard again in guns
Thundering on the ridge and from the hills
Over the looted farms and burned-out homesteads,
And heard in Jackson's holy battle cry.

You and your father fought us well, indeed,
In your far post in London, where words were
   weapons.
But you did not face iron shot, breathe smoke,
Smell blood, nor ever see the tortured look,
Or the triumphant stillness on the faces
Of boys like Alston, or men whose children looked
To that stillness for their heritage. If now
My stillness comes, my time for timelessness,
I welcome it and laugh to think that death
Who would not gather me with Jackson's harvests
Beside the Shenandoah, nor at Gaines' Mill
With my fierce Tiger Wheat, nor in my triumph
At Mansfield, near to my home, with modest
   Mouton,
Nor on Red River with kindly Thomas Green,
Death, now in this foul Fair of Vanities
Ferrets me out, flailing my flesh again
With my old sickness. Yet, if it take me there,
Where Mimi is and my dear Zack and Dixie,
My mother and my noble father, and his,
Where Jackson surely is and where, perhaps,
Surprising Apollyon, some of my Tigers are,
I shall not go unwillingly. If I
Could wish for you, I should wish such a death.

CROSSING THE PEDREGAL

pedregal: "a stonie place"

If we abandon our position, . . . what will you
do? Will you remain or leave the city?
—R. E. Lee to Mary Custis Lee, February 21, 1865

Richmond, April 3, 1865

    The odor of charred embers penetrates
My shuttered room, mingling with that of spring's
First opened roses, valiant in their brave show
As were my daughters, when the enemy came,
New-blossomed roses, piercing the heart with loss,
More grief than one so old as I can bear.
The Federal foot, booted and spurred, again
Has set its bloody heel upon my threshold,
Dominion over the Old Dominion forced,
As once before they entered Arlington,
And power supreme dismisses courage and skill,
Undoes all gains. Their guns, always their guns
More and more powerful than ours.

    Richmond has fallen, its heart caught up in
flame, Warehouses, mills, arsenals, armories,
All fired by Ewell's men in their withdrawal—
And even Custis shares this demolition—
Exigencies of war, the terrible waste.
All night shells scattered an iron hail, in random
Volleys of sound, worse than a battlefield,
The rattle of cartridges like musketry,
Explosions feeding on the exploding powder.

Nearer, at times, I heard the roar of flames
As houses, the shabby with the beautiful,
Caught fire, while helpless tenants watched them
    burn.
The church near me, and then a neighbor's house,
And once my roof flared up—a wind-blown brand
That God and a precious loyal hand put out.
Meanwhile, I'm told, a starving mob has stormed
The opened commissaries, a drunken rabble
Of whites and blacks alike looting the shops,
Government offices, abandoned homes.

      Near dawn, there came the worst, as Admiral
    Semmes
Withdrew, with him, our little Navy, brave,
But helpless. Our gunboats, rams, and ironclads,
Fired by their crews, exploded, shook the city,
A manmade tremor of the earth itself.
At daylight Gary's rearguard cavalry
Clattered through streets littered with looted goods,
With chimney bricks, burned documents, charred
    beams,
And shattered glass, crowded with women and
    children,
The homeless old and sick, the straggler scum.
On orders, he left the city to surrender—
James River's high-arched bridges arcs of flame.
This afternoon seems now a twilight darkness,
A pall of blackened smoke veiling the sun.
Weitzel, I'm told, commands the city. And I,
As your wife, must endure a Federal guard.

When this, the bitterest campaign, began
With March's warmth and urgent blossoming,
All I could think of, Robert, was my loss,
My home, the woods and gardens of Arlington,
My mother's, mine, my daughters'. Each in turn,
Digging and planting, made the earth our own:
The white and purple crocus earliest,
Violets, then jonquils, later the yellow jasmine,
My mother's trellised arbor beyond the garden,
Suffusing the warm spring air with its pure fragrance;
And roses, always roses, for you to gather
And set beside each lady's place. In earth,
Where now mound up the alien soldiers' graves,
Never again, I feared, would I see crocus
Lighten a corner of a young girl's garden,
Nor ever again the graves of mother and father,
Nor ever the mound where their dear nurse and
    mine
Is buried, Nannie, so old she knew Mt. Vernon.
I would not see again my childhood home,
Rooms of my children's births, each private place,
Large rooms for large and lovely boys to romp in,
With laughter and sometimes tears. And, oh, ironic,
Remembering the Fourth, gathered in darkness
All of us, in the high set portico
To see the fireworks at the Capitol,
Bursting beyond the river, our sacred ritual,
The children's and servants' awed, astonished cries.

These simple things that are a woman's being
Shape and are shaped by her to nourish souls.
To these my spirit clings because we live,

Dwell, by necessity, with simple things
Until the things themselves become our tokens
Of lives lived well and thoughtfully with others,
Symbolic, sacred to me and those I love.

You know the little I could take I lost,
For from each refuge I was driven again,
From Ravensworth, from Fitzhugh's farm and
   orchard,
The old White House my father cherished so
As the loved wedding place of the great soldier,
Now burned irrevocably by vandal soldiers.
If I regretted the loss of gardens and rooms,
Arbors and intimate places, my woman's being
In things one cares for, pictures and books, a plate,
Even a spoon that my dear mother gave me,
If bitterly I regretted and repined,
Hated implacably the enemy,
Who, then, Robert, could say me nay, who answer?
I settled in this rented house, at last,
Writing you I would not again be driven,
Would not again flee from the Federal heel.

I have not borne my sufferings as I should,
As you, I know, would have me bear them. I
Could not, like you, make suffering a virtue.
Death for the soldier strips his soul and name
Of the ignoble, trivial, and unjust,
While I have borne the mundane day until
Through gradual loss of motion, insidiously
The long encroachment of my daily pain
Conquers me while I cannot strike at it.

Mine is no public effort amid one's peers
But solitary, homebound, sheer endurance
Until, unwilled, my soul fell into disorder,
Despair, and almost infidelity,
Till death seemed not a challenge but escape,
Like the wounded man, lying in helpless pain
On the red field, who begs of friend or foe
The mercy of a bullet.

                         It seemed I had failed utterly.
    At times
My very words of prayer quivered and vanished
And in my head dry silence supervened,
A vacancy to match the vacant sky.
And I seemed lost in a desert not of the saints,
Seemed wandering in a wilderness alone.
Perhaps my enemy was fatigue, perhaps
The irrational increment of helpless days,
Deadly with loss that only found renewal
In hope of retribution.

                         My rage was deeper
Precisely because it had no means of action.
You spend your wrath in battle while I cannot,
And if you fall, you always have your men,
Who will keep bright the flame of your repute,
Whether we win or lose our independence.
Why, what have I to do these long dull hours
But knit and hear of you and the brave men
You have infused with your strong stoic will,
Aurelius's patience and Roman dignity,
With more success than you have had with me
Or my reluctant will.

You said to me when Edward fell at Belmont,
Mortally wounded, far from home and kin
That "All must suffer." Again, when even you
Could scarcely pray, you bore our Annie's death,
Then Charlotte's and her children's, saying to me
That reason and faith are all that we are given,
That what we cannot change we must endure.
But where is reason, when evil alternatives
Leave all that is dear to us destroyed and we
Are prisoners, subject to their naked power?
Yet now you write to me of General Hill
That he is dead, that "He is now at rest,
And we who remain must be the ones to suffer."
"All must suffer," and so, Robert, you say,
Trying to guide me to your patient way.

And yet, and yet. There may yet be a change,
If any change of spirit, by means as simple
As memory and reflection may be conclusive.

You sent me, for diversion I am sure,
Last week, old General Scott's recent memoir.
Reading in it at times, while hearing always
The thunder of bombardment south of Richmond
And fainter, Petersburg, eager to find
Whether he honors still his Southern men,
How he recalls your time in Mexico,
I found he writes of your reconnoissance
South of the City of Mexico, scouting
The lava field they called the Pedregal.
And I recalled the day that you returned
To us, who loved you so, our hero and father,

As if not seventeen years had passed. Then I
Remembered, too, how you regaled the boys,
Custis, Fitzhugh, and even little Rob,
With stories I half heard above their laughter
Of stubborn Mexican mules and fierce wild pigs,
But that strange tale they quieted to hear—
Of the task that you were given, Scott's engineer,
To find a passage through the Pedregal,
The pathless waste Worth deemed impassable,
That Mexicans, questioned, called the "Devil's
      place."
Indeed, like the world, it proved the devil's place,
Most like an ice field, fissured by deep crevasses,
Or like a storm-tossed sea, congealed in motion.
High ridges, sharp rock, broken and creviced stones
Gave no smooth surface for steady footing, or place
From which to look beyond. Missteps were painful.
It was, you told your sons, like Jeremy's desert
Or Bunyan's Valley of the Shadow of Death.

      Yet you, on your first scout, stumbling and
  falling,
Searching for open ground, found out a trace,
Faint signs where Indians, Aztecs, perhaps, had
  gone:
A rock moved slightly here, and there, two stones
Placed near each other, and so you reached the
  edge,
The hill Zacatepec. From there you saw
Valencia's men beyond, encamped to guard
San Angel Road. You noted their defense,
Returned again, crossing the jagged field,

Reported to Scott. Next dawn, with pioneers,
Who cleared and widened it for infantry,
You guided guns and horsemen to positions,
And stayed to aid in their artillery duel,
Then moved beyond Zacatepec, a ravine,
The road, to set a line above Contreras.
Yet, late that night, in driving wind and rain,
Dark save for lightning of a sudden storm,
You and a few bold men, hand held in hand,
Waded the ravine, rain-swollen, turbulent,
Recrossed the stony field, found General Scott,
And reported. Again, a third time, he sent you,
Sleepless in darkness, carrying urgent orders
For the attack at dawn above Contreras.
Still that same day, you guided Pierce's and Shields's
Bloody attack at Churubusco. A day,
A night, a second day of sleepless duty.

      Hearing this strange war tale your wide-eyed
   sons
Took in the meaning as you meant they should:
Given a task, whether there follow pain,
Suffering, cold, fatigue, uncertainty,
The path seem almost imperceptible,
When wading a swollen stream, your only safety
A hand to grasp lest you be swept away,
Your comfort, a glance of praise for work well done
Or cup of coffee in a lamplit tent,
Crossing the Pedregal seems life itself.

      So, now, remembering, I may conceive
My task in terms of yours so long ago:

To follow an ancient trace when there seems none
And no light given; to push on through the dark,
Knowing the right direction against the wind;
Simply to keep on at the given task,
Its time and place set by God's providence,
And claim no room, no garden as my own.
I think now I can wait His will, and yours,
Robert, whether there come our victory,
Defeat, or prison or long-protracted trial,
Or even exile. If faith's light darken down
To nothingness, I know it will flame up
Some time, some place along the jagged way,
Casting a shaded light within a quiet room.

IV
BRIGHT FICTIONS

ON AN EARLY CYCLADIC HARPIST (2600-2500 B.C.) IN THE J. PAUL GETTY MUSEUM

Oval the sweep, the motion horizontal.
The arched harp seems the entrance to a world
Where sunlight falls on singing faces, arms
Uplifted—instrumental to mused charms.
He listens. Then, singing, hears his contrapuntal
New variations on ancestral glories.
Seeing is hearing, hearing touch, sometimes,
Some places. Enter where, immemorially,
Memory holds, sifting, the unlost stories.

ON AN EARLY CYCLADIC HARPIST (2500 B.C.) IN THE ARCHAEOLOGICAL MUSEUM IN ATHENS

A geometric form, seated, erect,
Face lifted, as if hearing each plucked note.
His broken arms yearn toward the absent strings.
Romantic notion! There was no longing there
For being's absence. In the tale he sings—
A hero's wrath examined, a woman's heart—
Words that compose the listener's soul reflect
Right order in his own. You were, and are,
Small harpist, art's embodiment of art.

ON AN ARCHAIC KOUROS (530-520 B.C.) IN THE J. PAUL GETTY MUSEUM

> *. . . divinity*
> *Discerns reserves of strength in men.*
> —Pindar *Isthmians* 5.12-13

Tall as a god and like the gods remote,
Their radiant touch, their holy energy,
Momently sensed in arms, thighs, knees and feet,
He gathers ancestral gifts, paternal devotion,
His youthful will in one daimonic motion—
The nexus where divine and human meet.
Apollo's *eros* storied in the stone.
Here, Pindar, in his silent step, emotion
I hear in you becomes, again, your own.

On an Attic Red-Figured Amphora (490 B.C.) by the "Berlin Painter" in the Metropolitan Museum

The one young singer, clay-red on sheer black,
Flings back his head in joy, advances dancing.
Drawn lines of kithara, khiton, sash, and back
Repeat the amphora's fictile lines, hold time
Controlled, almost, in space's turned dimension.
His will, Apollo's now, seeks the sublime.
Archaic art. Yet clarity and tension
Seem threatened by the singer's imminent rapture.
Quest for the god, young soul, might prove your
　　capture.

ON AN ATTIC RED-FIGURED KYLIX DEPICTING OEDIPUS AND THE SPHINX (470 B.C.) BY THE "OEDIPUS PAINTER" IN THE VATICAN COLLECTIONS

Superb in clarity and confidence,
A cross-legged traveler, he sits at ease.
His thinker's pose, ironically conceived,
Is subtly touched with dubious innocence.
That riddle solved won Thebes. Yet, who that raised
This wine-cup to the gods would not remember,
Oedipus, your quick rage where three roads crossed,
Iokasta's cry, your blindness, and then see
The riddle of divine veracity?

ON THE JAMB-STATUES OF THE PORTAIL ROYAL (1150) OF CHARTRES CATHEDRAL

Kings, queens of Judah, patriarchs, prophets, saints
Yield in their solemnly molded stone constraints
To no one's freedom. For their fluent Word,
Distinguished, still is part of that to be.
God of Abraham, Isaac, Jacob, help
Here in the stone-flesh other men to see
Imaged an emblem of fidelity,
Which is no dream, but hope illuminate,
And love, resisting hell, able to wait.

ON THE VIRGIN AND CHILD CARVED IN OAK (AUVERGNE, 1150-1200) IN THE METROPOLITAN MUSEUM

A single form, they sit in majesty—
His face and hers identical in feature.
Their simple robes compose a symmetry
In folds like those wind-carven sand assumes.
Immaculate again, the human creature,
Austere and almost arrogant, resumes,
Now full of grace, the hope of human solace.
Dreamers, whose curious steps invade these rooms,
Carry the image with you. It holds promise.

ON DIERIC BOUTS'S *VIRGIN AND CHILD* (1460) IN
THE CALIFORNIA PALACE OF THE LEGION OF HONOR
For Erica

Timeless the pose as yesterday's caress.
His lips touch hers, his hand her breast. Eyes
    lowered,
Her slender fingers cradle his nakedness:
Innocence in an intimate communion.
Now when I see you hold your newborn son
As if the same sight filled your eyes, I bless
Whatever keeps us so. Although some say
Lust informs all love, others say grace ranges
Downward, perfecting love through all its changes.

ON DÜRER'S ENGRAVING OF *PILATE WASHING HIS HANDS* (1512)

Arrogant young flesh kneels to his calm power,
Proffering ewer and laver. This world's prince,
Impassive Pilate listens to whispered slander.
One, leading Jesus off, looks back in doubt.
Familiar faces, known in every time,
They think too much of life and not of death.
The present claims them wholly. Your word seems
Too hard for them: that still your kingdom is,
Still, though men fill the earth, not of this world.

ON BREUGHEL THE ELDER'S *THE HARVESTERS* (1565) IN THE METROPOLITAN MUSEUM

Little thanksgiving here. To labor, feed,
Quickly, to sleep, rise, scythe and gather grain—
The swathe and shocks still to be done again—
Leaves only the blunt will to survive and breed.
Fatigue, deep as disease, maims mind and bone.
Such work-dulled eyes and gestures I have known.
My Celtic folk, brothers to these, do you
Rest well, incorporate with the crops you grew,
Or do you live in me, singing now—in my ease?

ON CARAVAGGIO'S *CONVERSION OF ST. PAUL* (1600) IN SANTA MARIA DEL POPOLO, ROME

For Thom Gunn

nec spe, nec metu

Darkness and light define here one another.
Not Saul, nor yet St. Paul, he sprawls between—
Eyes shut, arms open, feeling but not yet seeing,
Wanting but not yet having what may follow.
Ambiguous interval. Here one might linger,
Not fearing and not hoping—would it stay!
But time and death are real. Light wanes or grows
To an extreme. You knew and raged. And hoped—
Painting as saints the sinners Christ loved best.

On Rembrandt's Etching *Joseph Telling His Dream* (1636)

Intelligence illuminates his face,
And youth, his beauty. Curious, ingenuous, he—
As if it were another's—tells his dream
Of sun and moon and stars bowed down to him.
Envy blurs wonder. Of the brothers, none,
Through faith or wit, can fathom unearned grace.
Yet, Judah, count yourself the lucky one:
You shall, through Joseph's guile, redeem yourself,
Given for Benjamin, to his embrace.

On Rembrandt's *Self-Portrait* (1658) in the Frick Museum

A luminescence thrusts aside the dark
To mold a hand and lip more real than mine—
Solid in presence, searching to contain
Or say some word, if only by suggestion.
All of your faces ask some question: Paul,
Bathsheba, Aristotle, old Dutch merchants,
Titus, Tobias; your many differing selves,
So constant in contemplative inquiry.
Is that your truth, simply to ask a question?

On Vermeer's *Young Woman with a Water Jug* (1658) in the Metropolitan Museum

Not Martha nor Diana—only a woman
Working alone, light falling through the casement
On forearms, yellow jacket, blue-white coif,
On a clear brow and eyes that look within.
She pauses in meditative quiet, conscious
That in her being, before her work resumes,
She sees and she is seen, knows and is known—
Thinking: "It is as if this precious light,
Uniting me and him who looks at me,

"Imaged the unsourced being, first and real,
That gives our being momently, our seeing
And what we see, knowing and what we know.
It is as if my task, privately done,
Its time and place not in the world's arena,
Showed truth beyond geography's fine maps
Or charts of the astronomer—truth needed
By him who paints me here in his bright fiction,
Alone, as he is too, and also not alone."

ON WATTEAU'S *PILGRIMAGE TO CYTHERA* (1717) IN THE LOUVRE

Not Compostela where these pilgrims journey.
As in ballet, gallant and belle arise,
Join hands and arms, and bearing staff and scrip,
Move toward the waiting rose-bedizened vessel
That amoretti guide and Amor's torch.
Venus looks on with laughter in her eyes.
Love's private joys publicly formalized,
Reasonable enchantment rules, lest we,
Otherwise, seem more beast than humankind.

One woman lingers while Cupid tugs her gown.
Bending her head to hear her lover's speech,
She lets her fingers on her fan disclose
Gentle complaisance as she seems to say,
"When I look up, my eyes will hold my heart
With all its claims, more than your love can reach,
Perhaps, but not Eve's guile for you to blame,
Nor Venus's innocent, amoral gift,
Only a woman caught by what caught you.

"Though in Commedia's plots, our roles are fixed—
Silvia and Florio, or Livia and Leander,
Counters in love's game, partners in pas de deux—
What we may say is free. So I from you
Ask more than a lover's plea—a man's response,
Self-conscious, meditated, open as mine.

The simplest of my sex finds your sex simple,
While I, amazed by love's power to subdue,
Wonder by what illusion you are moved,

"Whether you want to love or to be loved,
Whether you need to know or to be known,
As I all these and more. Although for you
The asking seems enough (your eyes say this),
When mine meet yours, what happens alters my
    being
Irrevocably. Part of my story ends.
I see the others enter on their way,
Light-hearted folk, easy to love and leave,
Regretting little, when Cythera's long day ends.

"For me my going will be like a charm,
Chosen deliberately, although I know
Warm hands grow cold, arms drop idly away.
The sky seems vague with promise, melancholy,
The freedom of the island evanescent.
Some pilgrims have seen saints, carried their touch
Homeward again to seal love's errant will.
If, when I close my options, you do not,
Nor wish to leave the game, where will we be?
And if I love you always, what can I say?"

ON JAN VAN HUYSUM'S *VASE OF FLOWERS* (1722) IN THE J. PAUL GETTY MUSEUM

> dum loquimur, fugerit invida aetas: carpe diem
> quam minimum credula postero.
> > Horace, *Odes*, I, xi

Dense icon of time's passing: hyacinth,
Primrose and tulips by blown roses, gentian
And morning glory, brief as dew. A fly
Climbs on the vase. Yet there Cupids entwine,
The Lover to the Woman seems to say,
"Beloved, our loss is forever. Come,
Touch me and I'll touch you more tenderly.
Let time, when love is over, have its way.
Here in its shadow we have our long day."

On G. B. Tiepolo's Etching *Adoration of the Magi* (1753) in the Stanford Museum

Plump cherubs ride the star-rays down to see
The Gentiles honor gentle Mary's child,
A tomb his seat, hay-thatch his canopy.
The oldest kneels. A younger waits. A third
Obscurely muffles his face in folds. Time past,
Time present, and Time future hint the Word,
Its timelessness, but fail to solemnize
The mood, as unpretentious as the child—
As you, Joseph, with sleepy, steadfast eyes.

On Goya's *Duel with Cudgels* (ca. 1820), "Black Painting" in the Prado

Uncertain light limns hills obscure and sere.
Mired in quicksand thick as the atmosphere,
Two unknown men, who may be son and father
Or riven brothers, raise bludgeons to each other.
Starkly avowed, this reign of rage and pride,
Of reason's dream become nightmare and graves,
Makes time thereafter, Goya, seem prophesied:
Heaven not brought down to earth as you dreamed,
    young,
But hell raised up, an open field for knaves.

ON THE SOUTHWORTH AND HAWES DAGUERREOTYPE OF MASSACHUSETTS SUPREME COURT CHIEF JUSTICE LEMUEL SHAW (1851)

> Little ween the snug cardplayers in the cabin of the
> responsibilities of the sleepless man on the bridge.
> Melville, *Billy Budd, Sailor*

The countenance is grave but graced by candor,
By warmth as well as amply reasoned thought,
Shadowing the eyes. Patient through years of
    slander—
For freeing slaves, at first, and then for not—
While Phillips, Parker, Sumner hunted devils,
And Yancey, Rhett, and Wise urged Southern
    empire,
You sought attainable good through human law,
Loving the "Higher." Like Melville's Vere, you saw
Your necessary judgment among evils.

ON FITZ HUGH LANE'S *SHIPS AND AN APPROACHING STORM, OWL'S HEAD, 1860* (1860)

> And storms are formed behind the storms we feel.
> Melville, "Misgivings" (1860)

A steely light shadows the white horizon.
A sloop, a schooner, and a brig far out
In rising foam already feel the gale.
Nearer in calmer water men furl sail,
Striving to save their full-rigged ship and boat.
So felt the States the onset of unreason.
Were they, rent by self-immolating hate,
Driven, as Melville earlier asked, by fate,
Fidelity, or will infatuate?

ON ERASTUS SALISBURY FIELD'S *THE ISRAELITES CROSSING THE RED SEA* (1863?)

> By day a cloud, by night a pillar of fire.
> Milton

> Mine eyes have seen the glory . . .
> Julia Ward Howe

Reflected in rose gleams on "crystal walls"
And in Egyptian stars falling behind,
God's angel in the flame goads on the herd—
Cattle, sheep, camels, men—a holy stampede—
Mystically led by Moses, Miriam, Aaron.
Invincible vision of the bond-slave's hope!
When love and justice fail, mark your success:
Offering sword-drawn for your lash-drawn blood,
Armies enter with you the Wilderness.

ON WINSLOW HOMER'S *THE GALE* IN THE WORCESTER MUSEUM

Aquamarine and pearl the turbulent shore.
Athwart the gale, the woman and her child
Seem strong enough—her arms robust and sure,
Her feet foursquare, and—bred of fisherfolk—
She challenges the ocean unbeguiled.
Green foam and white frame a heroic vision:
An agon sensed of common humankind
Without transcendence. Homer, did you find
Our limit nature? Or was it your decision?

ON WINSLOW HOMER'S *MOONLIGHT ON WATER* (1895) IN THE LOS ANGELES COUNTY MUSEUM OF ART

Two seated lovers form one shadow, dark
But warmly intimate against the bright
Instants of surf that strike the blackrock shore.
Secure, they take the sea's luminous beauty
Into their joy, as if long-ebbing love,
Its power held back by fear (as you once painted
Two on a moonlit beach, separate, silent),
Had flowed, finally, into oneness here.
Their single, quiet form resists the many.

ON BLAKELOCK'S *MOONLIT LANDSCAPE* IN THE DE YOUNG MUSEUM

Tree silhouettes of hickory and oak
In mounded blackness spread against the light,
Yielding to monochrome one half the night,
While all the other has the lucent look
Of moon-engendered mist in open height
On shimmeringly unfolded lake and stream.
At Jasper once the Athabasca shone
With beauty like this, and so pure, I own
Your madness seems, for such, not too extreme.

ON GARI MELCHERS'S *WRITING* (1905) IN THE LOS ANGELES COUNTY MUSEUM OF ART

The house was quiet and the world was calm.
                    Wallace Stevens

How often did she make such quiet, one wonders,
This woman writing at a covered table—
Full summer light warming the roseate hues,
Mauve, red, and pink of dress and cloth and room.
A Wedgwood pier glass shows three Roman figures
In ritual dance—cool neoclassic Graces—
Beside a clay pot of geraniums.
Her taste eclectic—like our modern lives—
Loving the past but settled in the living,

She seems meticulous—even, perhaps,
Like Edith Wharton, passionate for order,
Feeling, as she did, that in house and novel,
"Order, the beauty even of Beauty is."
Stevens, though you sought order in the sea
And grander heavens, the threat of nothingness
Unmanned you. Most women have no time for such,
For fate constrains them to immediate means,
The quiet art of keeping calm the house.

ON DOROTHEA LANGE'S PHOTOGRAPH
MIGRANT MOTHER (1936)
To my aunt Nora

Remembering your face, I see it here,
Eyes weary, unexpectant, unresigned.
Not wise, but self-composed and self-contained,
And not self-pitying, you knew how to give
And when to take and, waiting, not despair.
During bitter years, when fear and anger broke
Men without work or property to shadows
(My childhood's world), you, like this living woman,
Endured, keeping your small space fresh and kind.

On Leonard Baskin's Etching
Benevolent Angel

I, too, have felt the fire of being burn
Till all my flesh and my mind, too, seemed ash,
And I as if I were not. There, at the turn
Of what is not and of what is, forms flash
Out of and into being. So, from black
Seemingly shapes itself your angel's white—
Arm, cheek, and plumage—while, equal in power,
Black eye and wing emerge ready for flight.
For both, the existential ground is bright.

ACKNOWLEDGMENTS

The author thanks the editors of the periodicals in which the following poems were published: "And Who is God?" in *The Epigrammatist* (1990); "Iraq: Abu Graib," and "Troy" and "Coronach for Christopher Drummond" in *The New Compass: A Critical Review* (2003 and 2004); "Metaphysical Song," and "On Taddeo di Bartolo's *Triptych of the Madonna and Child with Angel Musicians, St. John the Baptist and St. Jerome* in *First Things* (2006 and 2014), and "The Old Poet: Margaret Preston Remembers" in *Sewanee Review* (2014)

We would also like to thank Ohio University Press, who generously and freely gave us permission to reprint poems originally published in *Taken in Faith* (2002).

59023813R00079

Made in the USA
Lexington, KY
22 December 2016